The Elements
▽△△▽

Amber Rune

One Printers Way
Altona, MB R0G 0B0
Canada

www.friesenpress.com

Copyright © 2024 by Amber Rune
First Edition — 2024

All rights reserved.

No part of this publication may be reproduced in any form, or by any means, electronic or mechanical, including photocopying, recording, or any information browsing, storage, or retrieval system, without permission in writing from FriesenPress.

ISBN
978-1-03-831129-0 (Hardcover)
978-1-03-831128-3 (Paperback)
978-1-03-831130-6 (eBook)

1. POETRY, SUBJECTS & THEMES, NATURE

Distributed to the trade by The Ingram Book Company

As we journey through the Elements,
remember our paths are unique to each of us
and what works for me may not work for you.
We are both right, as we follow our hearts,
letting them lead us back to the Divine.

Earth . . .

ground energy rising
through valleys winding
ancient standing stones
doorways to worlds unknown
pebbles on the beach
magick within reach
sacred mountains to ascend
roots of trees twist and bend
plants and gardens grow
seeds we scatter and sow
dark forests and darker caves
finding crystals through blessed ways
dancing free in secret groves
Earth is a mystical treasure trove

flowers and shadows on display
labyrinths lead the way
finding elemental Gnomes
'round the ancient stone

all is dark and hidden
magick no longer forbidden
stars out bright
the time is deep night

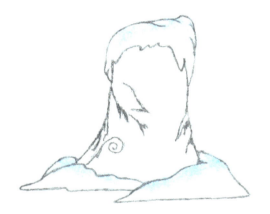

the darkest time of year
wrapped within a cold sphere
when the land shivers
the season is Winter

resting in the cauldron's embrace
creating dreams within your space
a time of reflection
north is the direction

protection, power, and fertility
magick around
Earth's symbol
the Pentacle is found

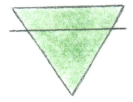

Air . . .

breathe again in rebirth
smoke rising from the hearth
air currents circle the land
smudging feather close at hand
clouds pattern the sky
leaves scatter and fly
storms spiral, surge and seek
echoes from high mountain peaks
sweeping across the plains
winds not always tame
all songs, all sounds
sacred chants within found
wisps of smoke reach divinity
Air is the dance of infinity

dancing amid the leaves
dew carried by the breeze
intertwined with every dream
elemental Sylphs hidden but seen

night fading away
new beginnings each day
colours a bewitching song
the time is dawn

days gaining length
flowers stir with strength
as returning birds sing
the season is Spring

everything returns again
awaken from your inner den
the journey released
the direction is east

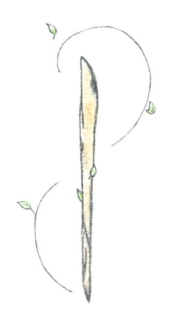

creativity, beginnings, and inspiration
magick around
Air's symbol
the Wand is found

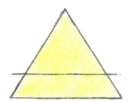

Fire . . .

balefires in the night
sparks rise, taking flight
illuminating sabbats' eve
a glow upon the web we weave
candle's meditating light
ancient stars twinkle bright
lanterns gently light the way
plants growing beneath sun's rays
stretched horizons of desert sands
volcanoes rise above the land
lava comes up from within
where all things must begin
burning in the dark
Fire is the eternal spark

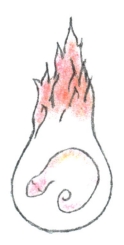

embers flare bright
holding off the night
when the spells flow
elemental Salamanders glow

everything radiant and bright
the world opens up to light
found at sun's peak shine
noon is the time

warm spells sparkle in the sun's rays
light taking over the longest days
bountiful land in colour
the season is Summer

travel your own road
the way the divine sowed
seeing all life's connections
south is the direction

transformation, passion, and energy
magick around
Fire's symbol
the Sword is found

26 —AMBER RUNE

Water . . .

rainbows circle the world
waterfalls cascade and swirl
secrets divine in the deep
our journey as we sleep
wishes cast to sacred wells
hidden calls within shells
storms upon us understand
rain restores the land
returning to the rivers and seas
waves become gentle, at ease
moon ruling tides
the ebb's flow and rise
mists spread past the shoals
Water is the oracle of the soul

waves crash the shore
alive with ancient lore
elemental Undines found
hidden in water all around

sky becoming art
when the night is at its start
colours merge into divine
sunset is the time

haunted days, harvest fun
with the slowly waning sun
as the leaves have fallen
the season is Autumn

never-ending night and day
the thinning veil, see the way
a transformation blessed
the direction is west

healing, dreams, and visions
magick around
Water's symbol
the Cup is found

Spirit . . .

from the edge of space
to your inner sacred place
the world filled with love
echoing high above
reflecting from below
as all the energies flow
weaving the web
as magick flows and ebbs
all elements as one
creating is never done
in the void of the dark
we clearly see our spark
the spiral path we create
Spirit is the journey of fate

nature's guardians still exist
seek them in the trees and mist
bringing messages and signs
like us, Elementals are divine

past and future unexplained
wisdom sought and wisdom gained
the cycle of day and night
time is an infinite rite

the wheel circles round
nature's rhythm found
everything transforms with reason
the time is every season

whatever way you go
a path which to grow
a magickal reflection
of all the directions

celestial, fate, and eternity
  magick around
  Spirit's symbol
  you are found

Your words. Your art. A space for you to create your magick.